A DAY IN THE LIFE OF A
Cross-Country Trucker

by Miriam Anne Bourne
Photography by Gayle Jann

Troll Associates

Library of Congress Cataloging in Publication Data

Bourne, Miriam Anne.
 A day in the life of a cross-country trucker.

 Summary: Follows a truck driver through his day as
he communicates with the dispatcher, inspects and loads
his truck for a cross-country trip, talks on the CB
radio, and makes rest stops.
 1. Truck drivers—Juvenile literature. [1. Truck
drivers. 2. Williams, Mike. 3. Truck driving.
4. Occupations] I. Jann, Gayle, ill. II. Title.
HD8039.M795B68   1988   388.3 '24 '02373   87-13582
ISBN 0-8167-1117-8 (lib. bdg.)
ISBN 0-8167-1118-6 (pbk.)

The author and publisher wish to thank Mike Williams, John Lubinski, Mike
Parks and the staff of Carretta Trucking Company for their help and coopera-
tion.

Mike Williams is a driver for a cross-country trucking company. He arrives at work with his bags packed, and walks past dozens of trucks in the company's parking lot. One of them will be Mike's home for the next week as he and his partner drive from New Jersey to California and back again.

Mike talks with the dispatcher about his assignment. He will be picking up a truckload of textbooks from an East Coast publisher and delivering them to a company in Los Angeles. The dispatcher gives him the papers on which to keep track of the trip.

Before Mike was hired, he had to pass a road test and medical tests. Like the other drivers, he takes a refresher course once a year. They practice defensive and winter driving, and they learn more about the engines of the huge trucks they use.

Mike locates the "tractor," or truck cab, that has been assigned to him. Some drivers have favorites, and spend their own money to install chrome trim to "customize" them. Mike stores his bag in an outside compartment on the tractor. Like other cross-country truckers, Mike travels with only a minimum amount of clothing and personal gear.

The trucking company's cross-country vehicles have a tractor that weighs 18,000 pounds and a trailer that is nine feet wide and forty-eight feet long. Smaller trucks are used for short-distance deliveries. Trailers that carry cosmetics are heated. Trucks that carry fruits and vegetables are equipped with refrigerator units.

When the trailer is not attached to a cab, the landing gear is lowered onto special concrete platforms in the parking lot. In warm weather, the asphalt paving can buckle under a trailer's weight. After Mike attaches the trailer to the cab, he uses a crank to raise the landing gear. Then the entire rig will be given a complete inspection.

Mike's partner helps make sure the truck is ready for the road. Is the electrical system okay? Are the lug nuts on the wheels tight? Have the lights and brakes been tested? On some roads, the mountain slopes are as long as fifty miles. The truck's brakes will be in use often on the way down.

In the company's garage, huge truck cabs are tipped forward so mechanics can get at their engines for repairs. Mike's cab has just had its regular maintenance, but the pre-trip inspection still takes about two hours. After the gas tank is filled, a computer is set to keep track of mileage and speed, and the truck is washed and waxed.

Mike fastens his seat belt and pulls out of the parking lot onto a busy highway. He would rather drive on the open road than in heavy city traffic, so he is looking forward to the wide open spaces further west. Mike's first stop will be a publisher's warehouse, where his empty trailer will be loaded with books.

At the warehouse, Mike backs the trailer up to the loading dock. This is a difficult maneuver, but he has a lot of experience. Mike is given a list of what they will be carrying. He must count carefully as the cartons of books are loaded onto the trailer with fork lifts.

When the loading has been completed, Mike and John again review the route they'll be taking on the first leg of the trip. Every state has its own highway regulations, so they must plan the trip carefully. One more stop must be made before the long-distance trip can get underway.

Mike and John take the loaded truck to a weighing station. Federal and state laws specify weight limits for various types of trucks traveling on highways. These restrictions protect the highways by reducing the need for costly maintenance. Several weigh-station stops will be necessary along the cross-country route.

Each axle of the truck must be weighed separately. The steering axle limit is lower than the limit for the other two axles. When the drive axle is on the scale, Mike can slide the wheels backward or forward by using a control in the cab. This redistributes the weight so the road requirements are met.

The truck is finally on the first of the cross-country roads. Mike checks out the CB radio, then settles into his power-controlled, air-ride seat and concentrates on his driving. Drivers who get good fuel mileage receive bonuses from the company. A "hubometer" on a wheel will accurately count the miles.

Hour after hour, Mike drives along the interstate highways. Cruise control helps him keep within the speed limit. Mike wonders if an observation service hired by the company is checking on his driving. The service reports whether or not safety rules are being followed.

At the end of the day, they pull off and stop at a diner for dinner. As Mike calls the office to report on road and weather conditions, John inspects the trailer's lock and seal. Hijacking is rare, but with a million dollars worth of cargo, they cannot afford to be careless.

While John takes a turn at the wheel, Mike "gets the house set up." He makes up the double bunk behind the seats in the cab. Mike and John will take turns sleeping and driving. Music from the AM/FM radio or from the tape deck will help them relax during the journey.

While Mike sleeps, John listens to other truck drivers talking over the CB. They have a language of their own. A toll station is called a "piggy bank," a tunnel is a "hole in the wall," and a bridge is a "gangplank." Mike and John will cross several gangplanks on their way west.

Mike takes over again after midnight. The next morning he and John take a close look at the clouds over the mountains. Mike checks a computer print-out he has brought along from the company's weather office. Although snow is possible in parts of the Rocky Mountains, they won't be there for another day.

UNSETTLED ACROSS PORTIONS OF THE ROCKIES AND GREAT BASIN

A STORM SYSTEM...CENTERED OVER SOUTHERN NEVADA...WAS BRINGING SCATTERED SHOWERS AND THUNDERSTORMS TO SECTIONS OF THE CENTRAL AND SOUTHERN ROCKIES AND SNOW TO PORTIONS OF THE GREAT BASIN. STRONG THUNDERSTORMS MOVED ACROSS EASTERN COLORADO THIS AFTERNOON AND DROPPED MARBLE SIZE HAIL THAT COVERED THE GROUND AT FALCON CO. SMALL HAIL ALSO FELL THIS EVENING AT CHEYENNE WY.

AN INCH OF NEW SNOW WAS MEASURED SUNDAY MORNING AT ELY NV...BUT THE SNOW HAS SINCE MELTED AS AFTERNOON TEMPERATURES CLIMBED INTO THE 40S ACROSS THE AREA. SOME SNOW IS POSSIBLE IN THE MOUNTAINS OF UTAH AND COLORADO AS THE STORM MOVES EASTWARD THROUGH THE CENTRAL ROCKIES MONDAY AND TUESDAY.

A HIGH WIND WARNING IS POSTED TONIGHT FOR THE WASATCH FRONT AND THE CACHE VALLEY OF NORTHERN UTAH. EASTERLY CANYON WINDS COULD GUST TO OVER 60 MPH TONIGHT IN SOME AREAS. THE WINDS WERE BEING CAUSED BY THE CIRCULATION OF AIR BETWEEN HIGH PRESSURE OVER WYOMING AND LOW PRESSURE OVER SOUTHERN NEVADA.

A LARGE HIGH PRESSURE SYSTEM OVER THE UPPER OHIO VALLEY BROUGHT FAIR WEATHER CONDITIONS TODAY ACROSS A LARGE PORTION OF THE NATION FROM THE PLAINS AND MISSISSIPPI VALLEY EASTWARD TO THE ATLANTIC SEABOARD. TEMPERATURES TONIGHT WILL BE ON THE COLD SIDE ACROSS SECTIONS OF THE SOUTHERN APPALACHIANS AND THE CAROLINAS. FROST AND FREEZE WARNINGS ARE IN EFFECT FOR MUCH OF SOUTH CAROLINA AND NORTHERN AND WESTERN NORTH CAROLINA.

AS OF 7 PM CDT...TEMPERATURES HAD ALREADY DROPPED INTO THE 40S ACROSS MUCH OF NEW ENGLAND...NEW YORK...PENNSYLVANIA...THE GREAT LAKES AND THE MID ATLANTIC STATES. WARMER 70S WERE STILL REPORTED ACROSS SOUTHERN PORTIONS OF FLORIDA...TEXAS AND THE DESERT SOUTHWEST.

HEAVIER RAINFALL DURING THE SIX HOURS ENDING AT 7 PM CDT INCLUDED A QUARTER OF AN INCH AT SANTA FE NM/.23/ AND AUSTIN NV/.18/.

...MORE...

06400300

Cross-country driving can be monotonous, especially on the interstate highways. But on some roads, scenic overlooks provide panoramic views of the countryside. So Mike and John sometimes stop along their route and enjoy the beautiful fall colors. Frequent rest stops also help them to stay alert, and to prevent highway fatigue.

Before getting underway again, Mike uses a heavy bar to thump the tires on each of the truck's eighteen wheels. A flat tire may look full because it is held up by the others in that row. If the bar bounces off, the tire is all right.

Then Mike checks the oil. The marking on the dip-stick indicates the level in the oil tank. If necessary, oil will be added the next time they stop for gas. Back behind the wheel, Mike pulls out carefully onto the road for the next leg of the trip.

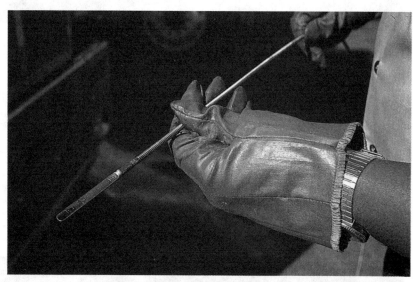

Mike drives the first part of the second night. Then, while John takes over behind the wheel, Mike climbs into the bunk and goes to sleep. A curtain between the bunk and the cab keeps out the lights and sounds of the highway. The roads are smoother during this middle part of the trip, so Mike sleeps well.

The next morning, they stop for breakfast at a diner that another driver has recommended. Truckers often use their CB radios to pass along information on good places to eat as well as information on traffic conditions and weather. On the road again, Mike stays within the speed limit.

Mike stops for gas at a place that is known for fast service. It takes forty-five minutes to fill both 135-gallon fuel tanks. Mike uses some of the time to make some entries in his log book. Inside the gas station, he and John study a map and trace the route they will be taking through the Southwest.

Some states require permits before heavy vehicles can use their roads. Mike has driven in every one of the continental United States. Sometimes, when it is his partner's turn to drive, Mike enjoys looking out the window at the changing scenery. He's often amazed at the different kinds of landscapes he sees, from one day to the next.

After dark, Mike shuts the curtain and watches television from the bunk. Each part of the cab has its own controls, so he can watch TV while John is listening to the radio up in the cab. Mike likes to listen to the radio, too, when he is doing the driving.

The next morning Mike backs the trailer up to the loading dock at the customer's warehouse. John checks in at the customer's shipping and receiving office. Once the truck has been unloaded and the cargo has been checked, the customer will sign for the delivery so the shipper has proof the cargo was received in good condition.

At the trucking company's Los Angeles office, information about the trip is collected from the computer. Mike shares a joke with John and one of the other drivers. A plaque on the wall lists drivers who have logged a million miles with the company. Each driver who has driven safely for five years is also awarded a gold ring.

After a few day's rest, Mike heads back East, carrying a load of electronic equipment. He takes pride in his job—transporting what people need. "I like being on the road," he says. "I'm at peace with the world while driving a truck."